10/8

TRUE OR FALSE?

The white circles in this photograph are ghosts.

TRUE!

At least, that's what many ghost hunters would say. They look at this picture and see what they call orbs—ghosts that are visible as balls of light.

FALSE!

Other people would say there are two possible explanations for these orbs. They were caused by light from the camera flash bouncing off dust or moisture in the air. Or someone added them to the picture.

In this case, the photographer used a computer program to create a fake ghost photo. But have some people been able to find and photo real ghosts? Read on to find out more.

Book design Red Herring Design/NYC
Supervising Editor: Jeffrey Nelson

Library of Congress Cataloging-in-Publication Data
Teitelbaum, Michael.
Ghosts : and real-life ghost hunters / by Michael Teitelbaum.
p. cm. — (24/7)
Includes bibliographical references.
ISBN-13: 978-0-531-12077-4 (lib. bdg.) 978-0-531-18740-1 (pbk.)
ISBN-10: 0-531-12077-5 (lib. bdg.) 0-531-18740-3 (pbk.)
1. Ghosts—Research—Methodology—Juvenile literature. I. Title. II. 24/7 (Franklin Watts)
BF1461.T3865 2006
133.1—dc22   2006006791

GHOSTS

And Real-Life Ghost Hunters

Michael Teitelbaum

WARNING: Do ghost stories give you the creeps? Do strange noises keep you up at night? If so, be warned. The stories in this book are true. Read at your own risk!

Franklin Watts
An Imprint of Scholastic Inc.
New York • Toronto • London • Auckland • Sydney
Mexico City • New Delhi • Hong Kong
Danbury, Connecticut

CONTENTS

GHOST-HUNTING 411

Get the 411 on ghost hunters' eerie investigations.

8
OVERHEARD AT AN INVESTIGATION
A Spirited Conversation

10
SEE FOR YOURSELF
A Gallery of Ghosts

14
WHO'S WHO?
The Ghost-Hunting Team

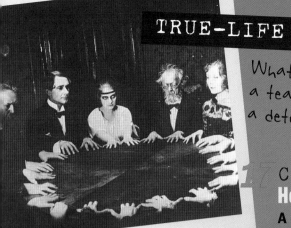

What do a famous magician, a team of ghost hunters, and a detective have in common?

Is this group contacting the dead—or being conned?

Case #1:
Houdini's Greatest Challenge

A century ago, mediums claimed they could contact the dead. Could the world's greatest magician prove they were lying?

Case #2:
The Most Haunted House?

Some say the Barnstable House is the most haunted place on Cape Cod. What will ghost hunters find when they investigate?

2

Will high-tech tools help this ghost hunter in Massachusetts?

Residents fled this Toronto house in terror—why?

Case #3:
Mackenzie's Ghost

Joe Nickell investigates paranormal events. Can he figure out what frightened the caretakers of an historical house?

Here's some more dead-on information about ghost hunting.

48 FLASHBACK
Key Dates in Ghost-Hunting History

RIPPED FROM THE HEADLINES **50**
In the News

52
CAREERS
Help Wanted: Psychologist

YELLOW PAGES

56 RESOURCES

59 DICTIONARY

62 INDEX

64 AUTHOR'S NOTE

Who do people call when they see ghostly sights and hear creepy noises? Ghost hunters!

GHOST-HUNTING 411

Ghost hunters search for the cause of the mysterious events. Is the house really haunted? Or is there some other explanation?

IN THIS SECTION:

▶ how to talk like a ghost hunter;

▶ ghost photos or fake photos?

▶ who is part of the investigating team?

A Spirited Conversation

Ghost hunters have their own way of talking. Find out what their vocabulary means.

investigation
(in-vest-uh-GAY-shun) a detailed search for clues and information

We've completed our **investigation** of your house.

Don't worry. We found no signs of **paranormal** activity.

paranormal
(PAIR-uh-NOR-mul) a way to describe unusual events or powers that can't currently be explained by science

Mice. Your house isn't **haunted**, but you've got a major mouse problem.

haunted
(HAWNT-ed) inhabited by ghosts

Say What?

Here's some other lingo ghost hunters might use.

> If you found **evidence** of ghosts, I'll have to move!

evidence
(EV-uh-duhnss) information and objects that help people make judgments or come to conclusions

> So what's causing those **eerie** sounds in the attic?

eerie
(IHR-ee) strange and frightening

apparition
(ap-uh-RIH-shun) a ghostly figure
*The **apparition** of an old woman appeared in the hall.*

medium
(MEE-dee-uhm) someone who claims to make contact with spirits of the dead
*The **medium** said he could speak with my dead grandmother.*

phenomena
(feh-NOM-uh-nah) events or things that can be seen, heard, or felt
*The unusual **phenomena** we witnessed made us wonder whether the house was haunted.*

EVP
(ee-vee-pee) EVP is short for *electronic voice phenomena,* recorded sounds and voices that investigators say are made by ghosts
*We heard the **EVP** when we listened to the tape, but not when we were recording.*

A Gallery of Ghosts

Did photographers use tricks to create these images? Or could the ghosts in these photos be real?

Ghostly figures have been showing up in photos ever since photography was invented. Most of the time, there's a perfectly good explanation for how they got there. Sometimes, dirt on the film or strange weather conditions caused ghostly images to appear in the photos. In other cases, photographers used tricks such as creating **double exposures**.

That's when a photographer—accidentally or on purpose—shot two images on the same piece of film. The final photo showed the second image **superimposed**—or on top of—the first image. And often the result was, well, ghostly.

Have a look at this collection of famous ghost photos. Some are obvious fakes. Others look convincing, but are they real?

Ghost Writer (1910)
A ghost inspires a writer.

About 100 years ago, followers of a movement called **Spiritualism** believed that some people could communicate with the dead—and even take pictures of them! But the images they took, called "spirit photos," were fakes. These photographers went out of business when their double exposures were exposed.

The Watertown Ghosts (1924)
Two ghostly faces bob in the waves.

Two sailors aboard the S.S. *Watertown* died as the ship was crossing the Pacific Ocean. The men were buried at sea. For the rest of the voyage, crew members said they saw the dead men's faces floating in the water. The captain took some photos and had them developed when he reached land. One of them seemed to show two ghostly faces in the water.

▼

Lady on the Stairs (1936)
A misty figure descends the stairs of an historic home.

People living in Raynham Hall in England reported seeing a ghost several times. They thought it was the ghost of a previous resident, Lady Dorothy Townshend. She died there in 1726, and her death may have been violent. According to some stories, she was pushed down the stairs.

In 1936, two photographers were taking photos of Raynham Hall. One noticed a misty figure on the stairs and pointed at it. The other saw nothing, but took a photo anyway. When the photo was developed, it showed a ghost coming down the stairs. Real or fake, this may be the most famous ghost photo ever. ➤

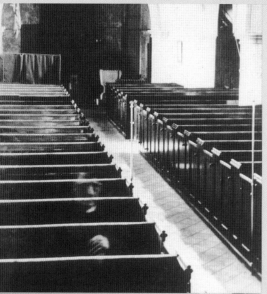

An Empty Church? (1956)
Who's that sitting in the front pew?

Mr. Bootman, an English bank manager, was shocked when his film came back from the photo lab. He was sure the church was empty when he took this picture. Had Mr. Bootman accidentally snapped a double exposure? ◄

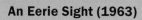

An Eerie Sight (1963)
A ghost in a hooded robe appears at an altar.

Reverend K. F. Lord took this photo of his church in England. Lord said he had noticed nothing unusual until the film was developed. ➤

A Ghostly Girl (1995)
The ghost of a young girl appears at a fire.

In 1677, a young girl accidentally caused a fire that destroyed the town of Wem, England. More than 300 years later, a fire broke out in the Wem town hall. A bystander took pictures of the burning building. He later noticed a ghostly girl in one of the photos. Was it the ghost of the accidental arsonist?

▼

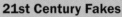

21st Century Fakes
Computer software makes it easy to create fake photos.

Today, people often use computer software to create ghostly photos. Photographers can easily alter images and blend them together to create photos like the one to the left.

◄

The Ghost-Hunting Team

Here's who might take part in a paranormal investigation.

EVP SPECIALISTS

They use audio equipment to try to record electronic voice phenomena (EVP). Many investigators believe that ghosts make sounds that can only be heard if they've been captured on tape.

INVESTIGATORS

They search for evidence of paranormal activity. Many use cameras to try to capture unusual activity on film or video.

RESEARCHERS

They look for historical information about the building that could help explain the mysterious phenomena.

LEAD INVESTIGATORS

They interview the people who have experienced the haunting and supervise the team on site. They also write reports about the team's discoveries and conclusions.

SENSITIVES

Some teams include people who claim they can sense the presence of ghosts.

CARPENTERS AND ELECTRICIANS

They inspect the building to make sure it has no structural or electrical problems that could be causing unexplained sights and sounds.

TECH TEAM MEMBERS

They're in charge of the team's equipment, which includes digital thermometers for finding cold spots and meters that can measure electromagnetic energy.

TRUE-LIFE CASE FILES!

24 hours a day, 7 days a week, 365 days a year, ghost hunters are looking for the causes of eerie sights and unexplained sounds.

IN THIS SECTION:

- ▶ how magician Harry Houdini exposed fake mediums;
- ▶ whether ghosts are haunting an old house in New England;
- ▶ and how investigator Joe Nickell solved the mystery of a famous haunted house.

Do You Believe in Ghosts?

Do you think there's a ghost at the top of these stairs—or are you skeptical?

When it comes to ghosts, there are three kinds of people: believers, skeptics, and disbelievers.

BELIEVERS

Believers tend to accept that ghosts are real. When they hear strange noises or see odd sights, they may be quick to assume that something's just come back from the dead.

And there are a lot of believers out there. According to a 2005 CBS poll, almost half of Americans believe that the dead can return in some form. And 22 percent claim they have seen or felt a ghostly presence.

Most ghost hunters believe in ghosts. During their investigations, they use special equipment that they say can detect the presence of ghosts. And in many cases, they claim to find measurable signs of paranormal activity. (You'll find out more about this kind of ghost hunter in Case #2.)

SKEPTICS AND DISBELIEVERS

Skeptics doubt that ghosts exist. They point out that there's no scientific evidence to support belief in the paranormal. Still, they try to remain open-minded on the subject. But disbelievers feel *sure* that ghosts can't be real.

Some ghost hunters are skeptics. They see reports of ghostly activity as mysteries to be solved. These investigators look for logical explanations for unexplained sights and sounds. (You'll find this kind of ghost hunter in Case #1 and Case #3.)

London, England
1919

Houdini's Greatest Challenge

A century ago, mediums claimed they could contact the dead. Could the world's greatest magician prove they were lying?

In the early 1900s, Harry Houdini was considered the greatest magician and escape artist in the world. He was also famous for his investigations of mediums—people who claimed they could communicate with the dead.

*Attempts to contact spirits took place at gatherings called **séances**. Séances were hosted by mediums, who charged a fee for their services. Houdini attended many of these gatherings in Europe and the United States. This story is based on true accounts, and combines events that took place at several different séances that he attended in 1919.*

A Spirit Appears

A woman thinks a medium has made contact with her dead husband. Houdini doesn't believe it.

A group of people entered the room and sat down at a round table. The only light came from a few flickering candles. The small London apartment was hot and stuffy, but no one cared. Their thoughts were on the séance that was about to begin. Would they succeed in contacting the dead?

The apartment belonged to the medium who was hosting the séance. One of the people at the table was a grieving widow. Her husband had recently died, and she desperately wanted to make contact with him. The widow had agreed to pay the medium well if she could put her in touch with him.

Séances like this one were popular in the early 1900s. At these gatherings, mediums claimed to communicate with spirits of the dead.

The medium asked everyone to hold hands, and the séance began.

The room was deathly quiet. Then the eerie silence was shattered by a sharp rapping sound: *knock-knock-knock*.

"Is this a spirit from beyond?" the medium asked. "If so, knock twice."

Knock-knock came the reply. The widow gasped.

"Prove to us that you are in this room," the medium commanded. A moment later, one end of the table rose a few inches off the floor.

The widow turned pale and nearly fainted.

"Now that we know there is a spirit in the room with us, we must prove it is your husband," the medium said. She handed a blank **slate** and piece of chalk to the widow. "Think of a question that only he could answer, and write the question on the slate."

"What is your mother's maiden name?" the

At some séances, people were stunned to see spirits appear. But skeptics said that mediums used stage tricks to create the ghostly figures.

widow said as she wrote down the question.

The medium took the slate and slipped it under the table. She held it tightly against the underside of the table with her fingers. Her thumbs stayed in plain view on top of the table.

After a few moments, the medium pulled the slate out from under the table. On one side was the widow's question. On the other side was a single word: "Hodgson."

The widow stared at the slate in shock. Then she began to cry. It was the correct answer. Her husband's spirit was there beside her!

Soon the medium said she was growing tired, and the séance ended. The widow hugged and thanked her. As she handed over the fee, she told the medium that she looked forward to many more séances.

Almost everyone at the séance that night believed that the medium had communicated with a ghost. But one man there wasn't convinced. His name was Harry Houdini.

Exposing Fakes

Houdini proves that mediums are fooling their customers.

At the time of this séance, Harry Houdini was the most famous magician in the world. He started his career doing card tricks and then moved on to bigger things. He once made an elephant disappear before the audience's eyes!

But it was his skill as an escape artist that made Houdini world famous. He could easily escape from jail cells and slip out of handcuffs. In 1912, he escaped from a locked wooden crate that had been wrapped in chains and lowered into a river. After that, his escapes became even more daring. In a popular trick called the Chinese Water Torture Cell, Houdini was hung upside down in a locked cabinet filled with water. He escaped in less than three minutes.

One of Houdini's friends was very interested in Spiritualism, a popular religious movement of the time. Spiritualists believed that people's spirits lived on after death and could communicate with the living through mediums.

Houdini attended a spiritualist séance with his friend—and became convinced that the medium at the event was a **fraud**. From then on, Houdini spent much of his time exposing fake mediums.

A promotional poster for Houdini's "Iron Can" escape trick.

Houdini prepares to dive into the water while chained to a heavy metal ball. Once underwater, he had to free himself before running out of air.

Houdini didn't deny the possibility that ghosts might exist. And he thought that if they *did* exist, it might be possible for a real medium to communicate with them.

But he was sure that none of the mediums he investigated were real. As a magician, he recognized their tricks. They were the same tricks he used on stage. He even began doing fake séances in his show so that people could see how mediums fooled the public.

Houdini had personal reasons for exposing mediums. He had been very close to his mother. After she died, in 1913, he missed her terribly. So he understood people who longed to communicate with loved ones they had lost. And he was furious that mediums took advantage of them.

Houdini hoped that he might some day find a real medium. He even offered a $10,000 award to anybody who could prove that he or she was really communicating with the dead.

Nobody ever collected the money.

A Secret Trapdoor

Houdini reveals the medium's tricks.

At the end of the séance in London, Houdini pulled the widow aside. He told her that she had been tricked by the medium. He also told her that he could produce exactly the same effects as the medium. The widow agreed to let him try.

The medium didn't protest. After all, that would just prove that she had something to hide.

Houdini asked the group to sit down again and join hands. "First we heard a rapping sound, correct?" Houdini asked.

The widow nodded.

A moment later, they heard the same knocking sound they had heard before.

"Then the table rose," Houdini said. "Like this." Suddenly, the end of the table closest to him lifted into the air.

"How did you do that?" the widow asked.

Houdini told her to look under the table. He showed her how he created the rapping sound by tapping his foot sharply against the table leg. Then he pointed to his left leg, which was crossed over his right leg at the knee. By using his left leg as a lever, Houdini was able to lift the table slightly with his knee.

"But what about the writing on the slate?" the widow asked.

"Ah, the slate," Houdini said, slipping from his

Harry Houdini, whose real name was Erich Weiss, stands next to his mother's grave. Houdini's sadness over her death led him to expose mediums who took advantage of people who were grieving.

This poster promised audiences the chance to see Houdini demonstrate how fake mediums fooled people.

chair and crawling under the table. The pattern on the rug was a series of rectangles. He lifted up one of the rectangles. It was a trapdoor! That section of the rug had been cut and glued to a small door in the floor.

Now Houdini reached through the trapdoor, grabbed a man's arm, and pulled him up into the room. Everyone stared at the man in shock.

Houdini explained that the man had been hiding under the floor, listening. When he heard the widow's question, he wrote it on a slate. Then he wrote the answer on the other side of that slate. He opened the trapdoor and replaced the slate the medium was holding with the one he had written on. The medium's thumbs, which were all the people at the table could see, never moved during the switch.

"But how did he know my mother-in-law's maiden name?" the widow asked.

"Simple," Houdini answered. "He read it here." He pulled a newspaper article out of his pocket. It was her husband's **obituary**, or death notice. The article gave the names of all his relatives. The medium had obviously given a copy of it to her assistant before the séance.

The medium returned the widow's money.

Because Houdini was so famous, people all over the world heard about his determination to expose mediums. Many scientists and politicians supported him. As a result of their combined efforts, the popularity of séances faded. And hundreds of fake mediums had to look for other ways to **con** people.

Houdini (*seated, at the right*) shows government officials a trick many mediums used. They made ghostly sounds by ringing a hidden bell with their feet.

DIRTY TRICKS
How did mediums fool their clients?

Fake mediums needed personal information about their clients to make their séances convincing. And they had lots of tricky methods for getting it. They read the birth, death, and marriage notices in newspapers. They took letters out of people's mailboxes. Then they steamed the letters open, read them, resealed them, and returned them.

They sometimes tapped phones so they could listen in on private conversations. They hired pickpockets to steal people's wallets and purses. They even sent spies to funerals to get information from the mourners about the person who had died. The mediums knew that there was a good chance that person's family would soon be giving them a call.

As Silent as the Grave

Houdini promised his wife that he would try to send her a message from the other side.

Houdini never found evidence that the living could communicate with the dead. Still, he promised his wife, Bess, that he would try to contact her after he died—if such a thing were possible. They created a secret code that he would use to send her a message.

Houdini died on Halloween, and Bess held séances on Halloween for ten years. No message from her husband ever arrived. At the final séance in 1936, she said, "I do not believe that Houdini can come back to me—or to anyone." Then she blew out a flame that she had kept burning since his death. "Goodnight, Harry," she said.

Magicians and fans still hold séances for Houdini each Halloween. They believe that if anybody could escape the silence of death, it would be him. But nobody has ever heard from Houdini. **24/7**

Magicians at a séance on Halloween, 1946, tried to contact Houdini. But nothing happened.

Harry Houdini never found evidence of ghosts. But some ghost hunters—like the ones in the next case—claim they have.

Barnstable, Cape Cod,
Massachusetts
June 9, 2007

The Most
Haunted House?

**Some say the Barnstable House
is the most haunted place on Cape
Cod. What will ghost hunters find
when they investigate?**

The Barnstable House

Psychics say they've counted 11 ghosts in this house!

Cape Cod is a narrow **peninsula** that sticks far out into the Atlantic Ocean. It has many historic towns and villages. It has beautiful beaches. And it has lots of ghosts.

At least, that's what people say.

Maybe the area's history has something to do with it. The Cape was settled by sailors and fishermen. Many of them were lost at sea and left behind grieving families. Other families suffered terrible losses due to fires, murders, and suicides. These are the kinds of tragic events that supposedly cause places to become haunted.

Built in 1713, the Barnstable House is one of the oldest houses on the Cape. During its early history, several tragic things happened there. One owner hanged himself. Another, Captain Grey, lost his wife and daughter while he was away at sea. The little girl accidentally drowned in the well. Overcome by grief, the captain's wife locked herself in a room on the third floor and died of starvation.

The Barnstable House, which is almost 300 years old, has a haunted history.

Many people believe that the captain and his family still haunt the house. During the 20th century, the house was run as an inn. Some

Does an old house in this small town on Cape Cod in Massachusetts really have ghosts?

guests reported seeing Captain Grey's ghost. They said he liked to slam doors. Other guests said they saw candles light themselves, or empty rocking chairs swaying back and forth.

In the 1970s, there was a fire in the building. Firefighters said that a woman appeared in a window on the third floor. But when they entered the building, it was empty. Later they saw a figure in a white gown floating above the front lawn.

Did smoke from the fire create the ghostly shape? Or had the firefighters seen the ghost of Captain Grey's wife?

People began calling the Barnstable House the most haunted house on the Cape. Psychics who visited the house said they counted 11 ghosts!

On June 9, 2007, a team of ghost hunters arrived at the Barnstable House to investigate. They wanted to see if all the stories were true.

They were amazed by what they found.

First Steps

Most ghostly events have logical explanations.

The ghost hunters belonged to a group called the New England Society of Paranormal Investigators (NESPI). It's one of many groups in the United States that investigate reports of ghosts and paranormal events.

Most ghost hunters don't get paid. They conduct investigations because they want to help people who say their houses are haunted. They also get excited at the chance of having encounters with ghosts.

Kay Owens is an investigator with the Scientific Investigation Ghost Hunting Team (S.I.G.H.T.) in Indiana. Like most ghost hunters, she believes in ghosts. But she says it's important to remain skeptical at the start of an investigation.

"Most cases can be explained as natural occurrences," says Owens. For example, a door can open by itself if it wasn't properly installed. A wet spot on a table can cause a glass to move by itself.

"Investigators should not go into a location thinking it is haunted," she says. "Ninety-eight percent of the time it is not."

Ghost hunters start by interviewing eyewitnesses. Then they inspect the site. They want to make sure there's no logical explanation for the unusual events—something like faulty wiring that could be causing lights to go on and off. When the inspection is over, the team sets up equipment that they believe can detect the presence of ghosts. (See page 32.)

Would NESPI's high-tech equipment detect any ghosts in the Barnstable House?

Ghost hunters Grant Wilson (*left*) and Jason Hawes set up equipment before an investigation. They appear on the TV show *Ghost Hunters*. (See page 50.)

A GHOST HUNTER'S TOOLBOX

Here's a checklist of a ghost hunter's most important tools.

DIGITAL THERMOMETERS: Investigators use digital thermometers to measure the temperature at many spots all over the site. They believe that cold spots may indicate the presence of ghosts. (There's no scientific proof of this.)

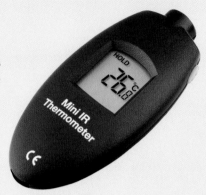

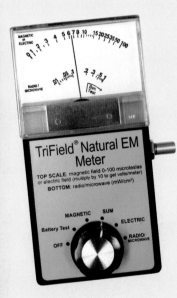

EMF (ELECTROMAGNETIC FIELD) METERS: An EMF meter measures **electromagnetic fields**. These invisible fields are made up of tiny, electrically charged particles. They're all around us.

Electromagnetic fields are measured in units called milligauss (mG). Most EMF readings are less than 2 mG. But the readings can be much higher around electrical wiring and appliances like microwaves. And if the EMF is measured near power lines, it can soar to about 100 mG.

Ghost hunters believe that ghosts are a form of energy and that their presence disturbs EMFs. So investigators use EMF meters to look for changes in the electromagnetic field. They think that a meter reading between 2 and 7 mG indicates that there's a ghost nearby. (There's no scientific proof of this, either.)

MOTION DETECTORS: Ghost hunters put these in rooms where ghost activity has been reported. Any movement will set off a signal that tells investigators to come take a closer look.

CAMERAS: Some investigators set up video cameras to record anything that happens at various places at the site. Many use digital cameras to take photos of places where they get unusual temperature or EMF readings. They think ghostly shapes may show up in the pictures.

AUDIO RECORDING DEVICES: Ghost hunters believe that some ghosts can speak or make other sounds. But they say that you have to record the sounds in order to hear them. Investigators use digital recorders to try to capture those sounds, which are called Electronic Voice Phenomena, or EVPs.

(EVPs are controversial. Most of these sounds are vague and hard to identify. Ghost hunters listening to an EVP they recorded might hear a voice saying "Go away!" But that doesn't mean you'll hear it, too.)

LAPTOP COMPUTERS: All the data from an investigation is collected on the team's computer. Investigators also use it for editing the audio and video material they record.

Investigator Jason Hawes unpacks his ghost-hunting equipment.

CRASH!

The investigation starts with a bang.

The NESPI team gathered in a large room. Several businesses have offices in the Barnstable House, and they use the room for meetings. Paintings of sailing ships decorate the walls. There's an old metal weather vane shaped like a whale on a stand in the corner.

The ghost hunters lit some candles. Investigator Mike Astin began by asking the spirit of Captain Grey to give them a sign that it was present.

Suddenly there was a loud crash. Everyone jumped. "What was that?" somebody cried. They looked around to see what had caused the noise.

The whale-shaped weathervane had crashed to the floor.

The ghost hunters stared at it in shock. "Well, *that* got our attention," Astin said. He thanked the spirit for showing its presence. Everyone laughed nervously.

Soon the team began their investigation. They sat quietly in each room, taking pictures and recording sounds. They tried to make contact with spirits by whispering questions such as, "What is your name?" They also took temperature and electromagnetic field readings—all of which turned out to be normal.

The room where Captain Grey's wife died was locked, but they were able to slide a microphone

Shortly after the ghost hunters gathered in the Barnstable House, this weather vane crashed to the floor. Did a ghost push it over?

into it. They managed to record several EVPs there. They also taped EVPs in other rooms.

For more information about EVPs, see the entry for "Audio Recording Devices" on page 33.

The ghost hunters said that when they listened to the EVP tapes, they could hear sounds they hadn't heard during the investigation. They heard faint voices saying things like "Help me!" and "When's dinner?" They also heard eerie whispering and humming sounds.

In one EVP, a ghostly voice supposedly interrupted two team members who were complaining that they couldn't find any light switches. "There are switches!" the voice called out. At least, that's what NESPI wrote in its report of the investigation. But EVPs are often hard to make out. Sometimes ghost hunters hear things on the tapes that other people don't.

Mike Astin is an audio and video technician by day and a ghost hunter by night. Here, he shows a client the results of a NESPI investigation.

NESPI's cameras captured nothing unusual that night. Still, based on the weather vane incident and the EVPs, the ghost hunters concluded that the Barnstable House was haunted. But they didn't feel that its ghosts wanted to harm people.

That didn't surprise Astin. He says that he has found that most ghosts tend to be playful. Maybe that's why he enjoys being a ghost hunter so much. "I love this," he told the *Falmouth Enterprise*, a local paper. "It gets my heart rate up."

Another Side to the Story

Did a ghost push the weather vane over? Or is there another explanation?

A ghost hunter searches for signs of paranormal activity.

Don Keeran works for an organization based in the Barnstable House. He says he once heard strange noises in his office. But it turned out that raccoons had moved into his bricked-up fireplace. Other than that, Keeran says he hasn't seen or heard anything ghostly. And neither have his co-workers.

He wasn't surprised to hear about the weather vane falling over. "It's usually propped in a corner because it will not stand up on its own," Keeran says. "It's too top-heavy."

Keeran has a **theory** for why he hasn't seen any ghosts. He thinks it's because he doesn't believe in them. "I suspect that people who are more likely to have ghostly things happen to them are the ones who already believe in ghosts," he says.

Most skeptics would agree. They say that people who believe in ghosts expect to find ghosts in so-called haunted houses. So any strange events are seen as signs of paranormal activity.

"Around these parts," Keeran says, "any old inn or bed-and-breakfast worth its salt has a ghost story attached to it." Haunted houses are part of Cape Cod's history. But do they really have ghosts in them?

It all depends on who you ask. 24/7

Toronto, Ontario, Canada
1956–1972

Mackenzie's Ghost

**Joe Nickell investigates
paranormal events. Can he
figure out what frightened
the caretakers of an historical
house in Toronto?**

Noises in the Night

The caretakers of Mackenzie House hear strange noises. Is the place haunted?

The Mackenzie House in Toronto is a popular tourist attraction. Is it popular with ghosts as well?

Mr. and Mrs. Edmunds lay in bed, staring up at the ceiling. A sound had awakened them, but now the house was silent. "It was nothing," Mr. Edmunds said. "Let's go back to sleep."

They were just drifting off when they heard it again—the sound of footsteps on the stairs. Somebody in heavy boots was climbing the steps. Mr. Edmunds jumped out of bed and ran into the hall. There was nobody on the stairs. He checked the whole building, but they were alone in the house.

It was August 1956. The Edmundses had recently moved in to the house. It was an historical building that was open to visitors during the day, and they had been hired as caretakers. The house had once belonged to a politician named William Lyon Mackenzie. In 1834, he became Toronto's first mayor. He was also the publisher of a newspaper called the *Colonial Advocate*.

A few nights later, they heard the sound of a piano being played. Mackenzie's old piano was in the living room, but they were alone in the house. Who could be playing it? By the time they got downstairs, the music had stopped.

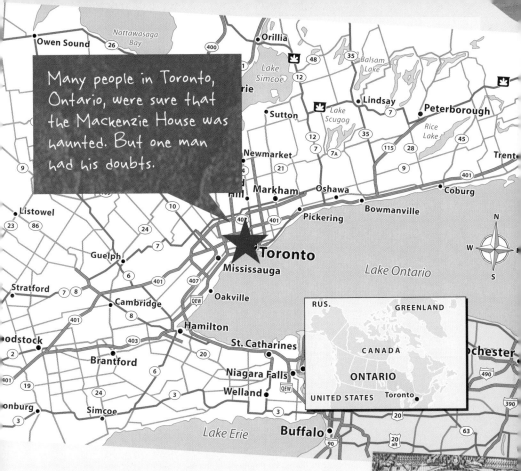

Many people in Toronto, Ontario, were sure that the Mackenzie House was haunted. But one man had his doubts.

The following week, the Edmundses were awakened by a strange rumbling sound. They checked the house from top to bottom but found nothing that could be causing the sound.

Mr. Edmunds said the sound reminded him of the clanking of old printing presses. They knew there was an old printing press in the basement. Mackenzie used to print his paper in the house. But the press was locked away and hadn't been used in more than a hundred years.

Over the next few years, the caretakers kept hearing the same mysterious sounds. And Mrs. Edmunds reported that she woke up several times to see a ghostly figure standing beside her.

W. L. Mackenzie lived in the house in the mid-1800s. Some people think his ghost haunts it to this day.

39

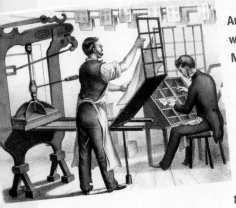

An old printing press like this one was locked in the basement. Was Mackenzie's ghost still using it?

By 1960, they had had enough. They quit their jobs and moved.

New caretakers, Mr. and Mrs. Dobban, moved in. They heard all the same sounds—the footsteps, the rumbling, and the piano. Within a month, the Dobbans were gone.

The Edmundses and the Dobbans told a local paper about their experiences. They said they were convinced the house was haunted. It became a famous Toronto landmark. As a real-life "haunted house," it was a popular place on Halloween.

But one man thought there must be another explanation for the eerie sounds the caretakers had heard. He decided to investigate.

Joe Nickell, P.I.

A detective decides to solve the mystery of Mackenzie House.

When Joe Nickell was a kid, he wanted to be a magician. He also wanted to be a detective. He grew up to be both.

After college, Nickell began his career as a magician. He worked at the Houdini Magical Hall of Fame in Canada and learned all about the

great magician's investigations of fake mediums.

A few years later, he also became a detective. He worked as a P.I., or private investigator, for a detective agency.

Eventually, the initials "P.I." took on another meaning for Nickell. He began working as a paranormal investigator. He was fascinated by mysteries of all kinds. Were psychic powers real? Did ghosts really exist? Or were there other ways to explain paranormal events?

Joe Nickell started out as a detective but soon began solving paranormal mysteries as well. He decided to find out what was really going on in the Mackenzie House.

In 1972, Nickell was living in Toronto, and had heard about the city's famous haunted house. Nobody lived there anymore, but tourists visited it every day.

Nickell was curious about Mackenzie House. He learned that ghost hunters had concluded that it was haunted. And he knew that its caretakers had been badly frightened. But was it really a ghost that had driven them out?

Nickell soon found a clue that something else might be going on. There was a publishing company right next door to the house! He wondered if its printing presses had caused the clanking sounds heard by the caretakers.

As it turned out, there were no presses in the

building. It housed the publisher's warehouse. But the seed of an idea had been planted in Nickell's mind. It was time for him to go see Mackenzie House for himself.

A Noisy Neighbor

Nickell investigates—and finds some answers.

Joe Nickell began his investigation by taking a tour of Mackenzie House. His guide said that she had never seen a ghost there. But she *had* heard mysterious footsteps on the stairs. She had investigated and realized that the sound was actually coming from the building next door. That's where the publishing company was located.

After the tour, Nickell headed next door. He met the superintendent—the man who took care of the building—and told him he was investigating the famous Mackenzie House ghost.

With a twinkle in his eye, the super said he knew all about the ghost. He led Nickell to the basement, and had him stand near the wall next to the Mackenzie House. Then he disappeared.

A short while later, Nickell heard a rattling and clanking sound.

The super returned, smiling. "It sounds like a printing press, right?" he said. Nickell nodded.

The super explained that he had simply turned on the boiler. As hot steam from the boiler rushed through the heating pipes, it caused them to knock and clank.

Nickell could tell that the sound was loud enough to be heard next door. He had no doubt that the noisy steam pipes were the source of the "printing press" sounds that had frightened the caretakers.

Next, the super took Nickell upstairs and showed him a set of iron steps. They were right next to the stairs in Mackenzie House. Climbing the steps made a loud echoing sound that could be heard in the bedroom next door.

The super told Nickell that night crews working at the publishing company sometimes used these stairs. It was their heavy footsteps that had terrified the caretakers.

And what about the mysterious piano music? Where had that come from?

The super explained that his family lived in an apartment upstairs. His son used to play the piano, and the sound would echo in an alley between the buildings. To people in the bedroom

Boilers heat up water to make steam for heating buildings. Nickell discovered that an old boiler like this one, not a ghost, had made the mysterious clanking sounds.

at the Mackenzie House, it sounded as though the music was coming from their living room.

Nickell thanked the super for his help. But he was puzzled. Why had the super never told anyone what he knew?

The super smiled. "Nobody ever asked me," he answered. Reporters had written about Mackenzie House, and ghost hunters had investigated it. But nobody had ever bothered to walk next door to talk to him.

The difference between Nickell and the others was simple. The reporters and ghost hunters had been looking for ghosts. Nickell had been looking for the truth.

WAKING DREAMS
People see strange things when they're half-awake.

Joe Nickell figured out where the mysterious sounds came from. But how did he explain the ghost that Mrs. Edmunds saw on several occasions?

Nickell knew she only saw the ghost right after waking up at night. Some people experience "waking dreams" when that happens. They think they're awake, but they're still partially asleep. In that state, people often see strange things—including ghostly figures.

Since her husband didn't see a ghost, Nickell thinks Mrs. Edmunds was just having waking dreams.

What Is Really Going On?

Nickell's approach is to ask lots of questions.

Nickell always starts his investigations by asking this simple question: "What is *really* going on here?" Then he tries to answer that question.

He never uses high-tech devices such as EMF meters. "The use of all this equipment is nonsense," Nickell says. "Unusual readings prove nothing. Besides, this equipment was never made to detect ghosts."

He also thinks it's silly to use tape recorders to try to capture ghostly voices. "If you believe that the spirit lives on [after death], do you also believe that the spirit keeps its voice box?" Nickell asks. "If not, how can it produce a voice?"

Nickell examines a fake ghost photo from the 1800s. He's looking for hard edges around the ghostly girl (*below, at left*) to see if she was cut out of another photo and added to the negative of this one.

Instead of using equipment, Nickell relies on his detective skills. He interviews people who have reported unusual experiences and asks them lots of questions. "It's no different than speaking to witnesses at a crime scene," he says. "I'm there to try to solve a mystery."

Nickell has investigated many mysteries during his 35 years as a paranormal investigator. And he says he approached each one with an open mind.

Joe Nickell in his office. He has written many books about his experiences as a paranormal investigator.

But so far Nickell has never found evidence of any paranormal activity. "I don't make fun of people who claim they've seen a ghost," he says. "I believe that they have experienced something that is real to them. I'm just trying to find out what that is." **24/7**

JUMPING TO CONCLUSIONS

There are unexplained noises in the attic. Does that mean the house is haunted?

It's human nature to want explanations for mysterious events. Let's say people hear strange noises in the attic but can't find the cause. Since they want an explanation, they decide a ghost is responsible.

Nickell calls that "arguing from ignorance." That's what people do when they come to a conclusion (*it must be a ghost*) based on a lack of information (*we couldn't find any other explanation*). The Mackenzie House case illustrates that kind of thinking.

To solve mysteries, Nickell says, you have to ask the right questions. And you should never jump to conclusions!

GHOST-HUNTING DOWNLOAD

Here's more dead-on information about ghost hunters past and present.

IN THIS SECTION:

▶ did three sisters really talk to the dead?

▶ ghost hunters who spent a year in a haunted house;

▶ why are these ghosts laughing?

▶ and America's favorite ghost hunters.

In the News

Read all about it! Ghost hunters are front-page news.

Ghost Hunters on Television

September 26, 2007

Tonight, a new season of *Ghost Hunters* starts on the Sci Fi Channel. The show features real-life ghost hunters Jason Hawes and Grant Wilson. The two men are the founders of TAPS, The Atlantic Paranormal Society.

By day, Hawes and Wilson are plumbers. At night, they investigate hauntings. And each week, the show takes viewers along on an investigation.

In one episode, they investigated some ruins in Ireland that were said to be haunted. "I started hearing various types of humming behind me," said Wilson. "And footsteps, and voices. That was something I'd never heard before. After a little while I could start to see little figures moving around."

What happened next? To find out, you'll have to watch the show.

Jason Hawes (*left*) and Grant Wilson (*right*) with other members of The Atlantic Paranormal Society ghost-hunting team.

Party Ghosts

NEVADA CITY, CALIFORNIA—July 6, 2007

Katie Bennett has been hearing strange sounds at the US Hotel ever since she took over the business five years ago. "The one sound I consistently hear is laughter," she told her local paper, *The Union*. She has also heard music and dancing.

Guests staying at the inn have also reported hearing strange sounds. And lights sometimes go on and off without anybody touching the switches.

Is the Inn Haunted?

Bennett's story caught the attention of NorCal Paranormal Investigators (NPI) from Sacramento. On June 24 and 25, the ghost-hunting team conducted an investigation.

The investigators recorded 50 hours of audio and videotape. No unusual images showed up on the videotape. But they said that their tape recorders captured some strange sounds. "We found some really good EVPs (electronic voice phenomena)," lead investigator Shane Thornton told *The Union*. He said that the recordings included a woman laughing and the sound of boots on a hardwood floor—even though the floors in the building are carpeted.

The inn was built in 1853, during the California Gold Rush. So is it haunted by the ghosts of people who once stayed there? Bennett thinks it's possible, but she's not afraid. After all, if there *are* ghosts in the inn, they seem to be happy and harmless.

The NorCal Paranormal Investigators pose outside the US Hotel in Nevada City.

HELP WANTED:
Psychologist

Meet a psychologist who studies why some people believe in the paranormal.

Q&A: JAMES ALCOCK, PHD

Dr. James Alcock is a professor of psychology at York University in Toronto, Canada.

24/7: What does a psychologist do?

DR. JAMES ALCOCK: A **psychologist** studies human behavior and experiences.

24/7: How can psychologists help in paranormal investigations?

DR. ALCOCK: Paranormal experiences are just that—experiences. Psychologists are experts in understanding the experiences that people report. By understanding these experiences, psychologists can help to rule out incorrect conclusions that something paranormal is happening when it is not.

24/7: How did you get interested in this aspect of psychology?

DR. ALCOCK: My major interest is in how people come to believe things, even in the absence of evidence. I became interested in reports of the paranormal because in those cases we have people believing things without any scientific evidence.

24/7: What types of careers are available to people who study psychology in school?

DR. ALCOCK: People can find work as researchers, school psychologists, or human resources personnel. Some psychologists work in hospitals, in schools, in advertising firms, or in large corporations. Others work in private practice, working with individual patients.

24/7: What advice would you give young people who may be interested in this field?

DR. ALCOCK: Make sure you work hard to keep your grades up. There is much competition to get into good college psychology programs.

24/7: How would a young person know whether he or she would make a good psychologist?

DR. ALCOCK: You need to have a great deal of curiosity about "what makes people tick." It is also helpful to be a caring person.

THE STATS

JOBS: You can't get a paying job as a ghost hunter. People who investigate paranormal activity work in a variety of professions. Some of them earn their livings as psychologists.

There are many different kinds of psychologists. Some of them teach at the college level. They do research at university laboratories and write articles and books about their work. Other psychologists work as **therapists**, helping people with problems. Sports psychologists deal with the mental factors that affect an athlete's performance.

MONEY: $40,000–$125,000.

EDUCATION: Jobs in psychology require at least four years of college. People who want to teach or do research need a master's or doctoral degree.

THE NUMBERS: The American Psychological Association has 148,000 members.

DO YOU HAVE WHAT IT TAKES?

Take this totally unscientific quiz to find out if being a psychologist might be a good career for you.

1 Do you ever wonder why people behave the way they do?

a) Yes. What could be better than trying to figure people out?

b) I only wonder about people when they act really weird.

c) To be honest, I don't think about other people very often.

2 Are you curious about people whose beliefs are different from yours?

a) I love trying to find out why people believe in certain things.

b) Not really. Everyone is entitled to his or her own opinion.

c) I like trying to convince people to share my beliefs.

3 Do you consider yourself a caring person?

a) Definitely. I care deeply about other people.

b) I care about the people closest to me.

c) I care when my favorite team loses. Does that count?

4 Do you have a lot of patience?

a) Tons. I'm a super-patient person.

b) Sometimes. But I don't like waiting around for other people.

c) How long before this quiz is over?

5 Do you consider yourself a skeptic?

a) I think it's very important to question things.

b) I don't always believe everything I hear.

c) I willingly accept the judgments made by people older and wiser than I am.

YOUR SCORE

Give yourself 3 points for every "a" you chose. Give yourself 2 points for every "b" you chose. Give yourself 1 point for every "c" you chose.

If you got **13–15 points**, you'd probably be a good psychologist.

If you got **10–12 points**, you might be a good psychologist.

If you got **5–9 points**, you might want to look at another career!

HOW TO GET STARTED...NOW!

It's never too early to start working toward your goals.

GET AN EDUCATION!

▶ Focus on your science, math, and language arts classes.

▶ Look at colleges with good psychology and science departments. (Psychology is the study of the mind and of human behavior.)

▶ Volunteer to help out at a community or health center, or at a youth or outreach program.

▶ Read anything you can find about psychology. Magazines are filled with interesting stories on psychological topics. See the books and Web sites in the Resources section on pages 56–58.

▶ Graduate from high school!

LEARN ABOUT OTHER JOBS IN THE FIELD

▶ child psychologist
▶ clinical psychologist
▶ criminal profiler
▶ forensic psychologist
▶ social worker
▶ sports psychologist
▶ therapist

NETWORK!

Talk to your school psychologist about his or her job. Ask him or her to put you in touch with other people working in the field of psychology, such as counselors and social workers.

GET AN INTERNSHIP

If you live in a college community, contact the psychology department. Ask whether they need interns.

Resources

Want to know more about ghosts and the people who look for them? Investigate these resources.

PROFESSIONAL ORGANIZATIONS

American Psychological Association
www.apa.org
750 First Street, NE
Washington, DC 20002
PHONE: 800-374-2721

This scientific and professional association represents psychology in the United States. It has 148,000 members, making it the largest psychological organization in the world.

Association for Psychological Science
www.psychologicalscience.org
1010 Vermont Avenue, NW
11th floor
Washington, DC 20005
PHONE: 202-783-2077

This nonprofit group is dedicated to the advancement of scientific psychology and its representation throughout the United States and the world.

The Committee for Skeptical Inquiry
www.csicop.org
Box 703
Amherst, NY 14226
PHONE: 716-636-1425

This nonprofit organization's mission is to encourage the critical investigation of paranormal claims from a responsible, scientific viewpoint. The Web site provides a broad archive of articles, features, and Web columns.

James Randi Educational Foundation
www.randi.org
201 SE 12th Street
Fort Lauderdale, FL 33316
PHONE: 954-467-1112

The goal of this nonprofit organization is to provide reliable information and promote critical thinking about paranormal and supernatural ideas.

WEB SITES

American Experience: Houdini
www.pbs.org/wgbh/amex/houdini

This PBS site provides information about Harry Houdini and a film about his life.

Borley Rectory
www.prairieghosts.com/brectory.html

Find out more about "The Most Haunted House in England."

The Fox Sisters
www.prairieghosts.com/foxsisters.html

Learn about these sisters who claimed to be mediums.

Ghost Haunts
www.ghosthaunts.com

This fun site offers a directory of haunted places and accounts of supposed encounters with ghosts.

Ghost Hunters
www.scifi.com/ghosthunters

Learn about the popular Sci Fi series and watch some of their episodes at this site.

Harry Price
www.harryprice.co.uk/index.html

This site provides information about the world-famous ghost hunter.

BOOKS

Banks, Cameron. *Ghostly Graveyards and Spooky Spots* (The History Channel Presents Haunted History). New York: Scholastic, 2004.

Costain, Meredith. *Hauntings Happen and Ghosts Get Grumpy* (It's True!). Toronto: Annick Press, 2006.

Dowswel, Paul, and Tony Allan. *True Ghost Stories.* Eveleth, Minn.: Usborne Books, 2003.

Gee, Joshua. *Encyclopedia Horrifica: The Terrifying TRUTH! About Vampires, Ghosts, Monsters, and More.* New York: Scholastic, 2007.

Hamilton, John. *Haunted Places* (The World of Horror). New York: ABDO and Daughters, 2007.

Krovatin, Christopher, ed. *The Best Ghost Stories Ever.* New York: Scholastic, 2004.

Watkins, Graham. *Ghosts and Poltergeists* (Unsolved Mysteries). New York: Rosen Publishing Group, 2002.

DVDS

Ghost Hunters: The Complete First Season. Big Vision, 2005.

Catch the first episodes of this reality show. The series follows two real-life ghost hunters as they investigate hauntings throughout the United States.

Unexplained: Hauntings. A&E Home Video, 2005.

This documentary from the History Channel explores the claims of people who say they've had encounters with ghosts.

Unsolved Mysteries: Ghosts. First Look Pictures, 2004.

Hear tales about curses and hauntings, friendly ghosts and historic ones, too.

Dictionary

A

apparition (ap-uh-RIH-shun) *noun* a ghostly figure

B

believers (bee-LEE-vurz) *noun* people who accept certain ideas and beliefs

C

con (kon) *verb* to trick someone

D

double exposures (DUH-bul ex-PO-zurez) *noun* photographs that combine two images on the same piece of film

E

eerie (IHR-ee) *adjective* strange and frightening

electromagnetic fields (eh-LEK-tro-mag-NEH-tik feeldz) *noun* invisible fields made up of tiny, electrically charged particles

evidence (EV-uh-duhnss) *noun* information and objects that help people make judgments or come to conclusions

EVP (ee-vee-pee) *noun* EVP is short for *electronic voice phenomena*, recorded sounds and voices that believers say belong to ghosts

F

fraud (frawd) *noun* a person who pretends to be something he or she is not, usually to trick others; a con artist

H

haunted (HAWNT-ed) *adjective* inhabited by ghosts

hoax (HOHX) *noun* an elaborate trick

I

investigation (in-vest-uh-GAY-shun) *noun* a detailed search for clues and information

M

medium (MEE-dee-uhm) *noun* someone who claims to be able to make contact with spirits of the dead

motion detectors (MO-shun duh-TEK-turz) *noun* devices that can detect movements in a given space

O

obituary (oh-BIT-choo-air-ee) *noun* a death notice, usually published in a newspaper or other publication

P

paranormal (PAIR-uh-NOR-mul) *adjective* a way to describe unusual events or amazing powers that can't be explained by current science

parapsychology (PAIR-uh-sye-KOHL-uh-jee) *noun* the study of paranormal activities

peninsula (puh-NIN-suh-la) *noun* an area of land that sticks out from a bigger piece of land and is almost completely surrounded by water

phenomena (feh-NOM-uh-nah) *noun* events or things that can be seen, heard, or felt

psychologist (sye-KOHL-uh-jist) *noun* a person who studies human behavior and experiences

S

séances (SAY-on-sez) *noun* gatherings during which a group of people try to communicate with the dead

sensitives (SEN-suh-tivz) *noun* people who claim they can sense the presence of ghosts

skeptics (SKEP-tiks) *noun* people who doubt or question ideas or beliefs

slate (slayt) *noun* a kind of tablet used for writing on; similar to a small chalkboard

Spiritualism (speer-ih-choo-wuh-LIH-zuhm) *noun* a system of belief or religious practice based on supposed communication with the spirits of the dead

superimposed (SOO-pur-im-POHZD) *adjective* describing something that appears on top of something else, such as a photograph in which one image has been placed over another

T

theory (THEE-uh-ree) *noun* a general idea used to explain how or why something happens

therapists (THAIR-uh-pists) *noun* people trained to provide treatment to patients with mental problems or psychological disorders

Index

Alcock, James, 52–53, *52*
American Psychological Association, 53
apparitions, 9, 10–13, *10, 11, 12, 13,* 16, *20,* 29, 33, 39, 44
Astin, Mike, 34, 35, *35*
audio recorders, 33, *33,* 45, 49, *49,* 50

Barnstable House, 28–30, *28, 29,* 31, 34–35, *34, 35,* 36
believers, 16
Bennett, Katie, 50
Bootman (bank manager), 12
Borley Rectory, 49, *49*

California Gold Rush, 50
cameras, 33, *33,* 35, 48, *48*
Cape Cod, Massachusetts, 28, *29, 35,* 36
carpenters, 14
Chinese Water Torture Cell trick, 21
Colonial Advocate newspaper, 38, 39
computers, 13, 33

digital thermometers, 32, *32*
Dobban family, 40
double exposures, 10, 11, 12

Edmunds family, 38–40, 44
education, 53, 55
electricians, 14
EMF (electromagnetic field) meters, 32, *32,* 33, 34, 45
equipment, 14, 16, 31, *31,* 32–33, *32, 33, 35,* 45, *45,* 48, *48,* 49, *49*
eeriness, 9, 12
evidence, 9, 16, 52
EVP (electronic voice phenomena), 9, 14, 33, 35, 50

EVP specialists, 14

Falmouth Enterprise newspaper, 35
flashlights, 32
Fox sisters, 48, *48*
fraud, 21

ghost hunters. See investigators.
Ghost Hunters television show, *31,* 50, *50*
Grey (captain), 28, 29, 34

hauntings, 8, 14, 28–30, *30–31,* 34–35, 36, 38–40, 41, 49, 50, 51
Hawes, Jason, *31, 33,* 50, *50*
Houdini, Bess, 26
Houdini, Harry, 18, 20, 21–22, *21, 22,* 23–25, *23, 24, 25,* 26, 40–41, 49, *49*
Houdini Magical Hall of Fame, 40–41

internships, 55
investigations, 8, 16, 18, 30–31, 33, 34–35, 41, 42, 45, 51, 52
investigators, 14, 16, 30–31, *31,* 32, 33, *33,* 34–35, *36,* 41, *41,* 44, 49, 50, *51,* 53
"Iron Can" trick, *21*

Keeran, Don, 36

lead investigators, 14
London, England, 18, 23, 48
Lord, K. F., 12

Mackenzie House, 38–40, *38, 39,* 41–42, 42–44, 46
Mackenzie, William Lyon, 38, *39*
mediums, 9, 18, 19, 20, 21, 22, 24–25, *24, 25,* 41, 49
milligauss (mG), 32
motion detectors, 33

New England Society of Paranormal Investigators (NESPI), 30, 31, 34–35

Nickell, Joe, 40–41, *41*, 42–44, 45–46, *45*, *46*
NorCal Paranormal Investigators (NPI), 51, *51*

Owens, Kay, 30–31

paranormal activity, 8, 36, *36*, 52, 53
personal information, 24, 25
phenomena, 9, 14, 33, 35, 50
photographs, 10–13, *10*, *11*, *12*, *13*, 14, 33, *45*
Price, Harry, 49
psychics, 30, 48, 49
psychologists, 52–53, *52*, 55

quiz, 54

Randi, James, 49
Raynham Hall, 12
red flashlights, 32
researchers, 14, 48, 53

S.S. *Watertown*, 11
salaries, 53
Scientific Investigation Ghost Hunting Team (S.I.G.H.T.), 30
séances, 18–20, *19*, *20*, 21–22, 23–25, 26
sensitives, 14
skeptics, 16, 36, 49
Society for Psychical Research, 48
"spirit photos," 11
Spiritualism, 11, 21

TAPS (The Atlantic Paranormal Society), 50
tech team members, 14
temperature, 32, 33, 34, *34*
Thornton, Shane, 50
Toronto, Ontario, 38, *38*, *39*, 40, 41
Townshend, Lady Dorothy, 12

Union newspaper, 51
US Hotel, 51

video recorders, 14, 33, 49, 50

"waking dreams," 44
Wem, England, 13
Wilson, Grant, *31*, 50, *50*

Author's Note

During my research for this book, I spoke with a number of fascinating and extremely helpful people. Specifically, I'd like to thank Loyd Auerbach of the Office of Paranormal Investigations in California and Joe Nickell of CSI (Committee for Skeptical Inquiry) for their great generosity.

I had a great time interviewing Joe Nickell. He presented an open-minded, logical approach to ghost hunting, and his common sense approach rang true. For example, he asked: "If a person can speak after death, does that mean that his or her voice box went to the other side along with the spirit?" I had never thought of it that way, but it made perfect sense (and made me laugh, too!).

This skeptical approach should serve as a guide to anyone who wants to investigate unexplained events. It also showed me the value of first-person sources and of speaking to as many experts on a subject as possible in order to get many points of view.

ACKNOWLEDGMENTS

Dr. James Alcock (York University, Toronto, Canada)
Mike Astin (New England Society of Paranormal Investigators)
Don Keeran (Association to Preserve Cape Cod)
Joe Nickell (Committee for Skeptical Inquiry)
Kay Owens (Scientific Investigation Ghost Hunting Team)

CONTENT ADVISER: Loyd Auerbach, Office of Paranormal Investigations